She Was

About the book

She Was collects three albums of lyrics - lyrics of call & response, of hope & disillusionment, of love & hate and of death & despair & damnation. The lyrics are inspired by the music of Vidulgi OoyoO, SmackSoft, RADWIMPS, Dismember, Runemagick, The Who, Rory Gallagher, Rainbow, Dio, Leonard Cohen, Deep Purple and Jethro Tull. They are a mixture of folk, shoegaze, (post) punk, (prog) rock and all kinds of metal. Written in English by j. t. baka in the years of 2013 and 2017 the pieces are located in the landscapes of Korean cities and... at sea - full of planes, pilots, mermaids, sirens and other creatures in, under, above and beyond heaven & hell.

About the author

j. t. baka published previously a couple of books under the pen names of Otaru Tomis and David Jordan. *She Was. Three Albums of English Lyrics* is his first publication in English only. Check out his website for more details about him and his books: https://otaru-tomis.jimdo.com.

j. t. baka

She Was

Three Albums of English Lyrics

Impressum

Redaktionsschluss: 21.05.2017.

Fotos : Simon Wagenschütz.

©2017
Herstellung und Verlag: BoD - Books on Demand, Norderstedt.

ISBN-13: 9783744822220.

Content

1st Album

Chrysalis & Orchid

--

2nd Album

The Prau

--

3rd Album

サクラ

1st Album

Chrysalis & Orchid

love's a cold turkey

butterfly's

feast

on St. Pain's

leaving

the future behind

trigger happy

Today

today i tried…

today

today i tried to

get…

today

today

i tried to get

lost

today

it didn't work

today

i failed

getting lost

today

time to move

on

to morrow

Then

i

was

more wet

than my umbrella

fuck

tomorrow

all smiles

die today

then

Time's Blend

a

love at the gate

breathing eyes

sucking dry

sucked by

time's

bleeding

there

tomorrowed by

hate

Tomorrow

came but never comes

todayed

then there

them

than me

as in as

of

yesterday

273

daydance

in

a daytrance

watching raindrops

rushing

by

the window like

tears

of

a butterfly

stonewalled

in your

heart

Thereafter

dreaming

clouds

dancing on sunrays

laughing while strafing

what's

dear and what's

near to the heart of

the matter

of

love

with what's

clouding

your mind

cloudlessnesslessnesscloudnesslessnessclou
dnesslesslessnessnessless

Today's Aftermath

not

tomorrow

yesterday

little orchid

today's tomorrow

happy

love shot

dreams of

an oxazepamed life

2nd Album

Musubi

Love Story

Anymore

I didn't stop the rain drops from

turning into tears.

I didn't stop the fire in my heart from

turning into ash.

I didn't stop your love from

turning into hate.

I didn't stop myself from

turning against us.

I let everything fall apart.

But I won't stop.

I won't stop the rain from falling.

I won't stop the fire from burning down

the house.

I won't stop you turning against me.

I won't stop.

Cause I can't.

Anyway

I couldn't stop me falling

in love.

I couldn't stop me searching

for more.

I couldn't stop me starting

to hate.

I couldn't stop me leaving

you.

Everything did happen. And I

couldn't stop any of it.

I couldn't stop. I just

couldn't stop.

Cause I didn't want to.

New Song

The Future

Back then

the future looked better,

they said.

I love you, you said

back then.

And I made love to you without loving you

back then.

And, of course, I left you

then.

Now

I am back.

And they were right:

The future looked better

back then.

I see it in your eyes.

the present

back

visiting parents

still

people in front of city hall

france burning

lost in flames

germany sacrificing-sanctifying herself for
herself

lost in good will

while

the media is lost in

TRUMPTRUMPTRUMPTRUMPTRUMPTRMP
RMPMPPUMPRUMP

lost in diversions

and yes

i see you

moved on without moving on

still

following your dreams

i see

still

lost in diversions

A Twosome Place

Move On

I didn't break the ice

because you were too hot to try.

I didn't cross the sound

because you were too quiet to try.

I didn't catch your eye

because I was too busy to try.

I didn't take action

because I wasn't the one you were

kissing

right then and there!

I didn't do anything (right)

although I should have.

Because it was time to move

on.

It was time to move on

and

on… to you.

Leaving Behind

I did try – I really

did.

I did my best – I really

did.

I did give you a chance – I really

did.

I did even wait – I really

did.

How ridiculous of me!

I did everything to get a second shot at it
after you moved out

of our future.

I really did.

But you didn't see, you
didn't understand.

You just moved on and left
me behind.

Another Twosome Place

Trials

I see you smile and

I smile back.

You say something nice and

I say something nice back.

I see you smile more and

I want to make you smile even

more so.

I see you more and

more smiling more and

more.

I can't stop trying to make you

smile,

to make you laugh.

I can't stop trying because I am afraid of

what's coming after.

I am afraid of losing the smile when I come
here to get my daily cup of coffee.

I am afraid of losing

you.

Plea (of a Future Trophy Wife)

I love your smile.

I love your eyes.

I love you making me laugh.

I love you making me love you.

I hate your smile.

I hate your eyes.

I hate you making me laugh.

I hate you making me love you.

Ihateyoumakingmewaitingforyourcourageto
kickinandtakeovertoconquer

ME.

Your prize.

Don't you see?

Don't you see how desperate I am?

Don't you see my sad smile?

I can't wait anymore, don't you see?

Why don't you see my sad smile?

Why don't you see how desperate I am?

Why don't you see

that it's

my last day

working here?

Into The Night

Doing The Math *or* **Hope**

Same you

Different me

Same me

Different place

Same place

Different people

Same people

Different lives

Same lives

Different story

Same story

Different ending

Same ending

Different you

Same you

Different ending

Same ending

Different story

Same story

Different lives

Same lives

Different people

Same people

Different place

Same place

Different me

Same me

Different you

Same you

Same me

Same place

Same people

Same lives

Same story

Same ending

Different you

Different me

Different place

Different people

Different lives

Different story

Different end-

Voice of _: Oh, come, you bloody fool! Don't fool yourself! Just get your act together and run for cover and pray it's not y-

Way Back

Going home.

Anticipating the turn of the road.

Anticipating the water and the tower.

Anticipating coming home.

Want to keep it easy.

Want to keep it simple.

Want to keep it safe and sound.

Anticipating the turn of the road.

Anticipating the water and the tower.

Anticipating what I left behind and is

still

there for me.

Want to keep it easy.

Want to keep it simple.

Want to keep me down.

Yet

anticipating what I left behind and is

still

there for me.

There for me to take

if I can stop me

from running away from

what I left behind and might be there for
me

still.

And might be there for me

still.

If I can face the music

that is

you.

Love Ghoul

I return home.

Oh, to my nice home!

I return home in my car.

Oh, in my nice car!

I return home to my family.

Oh, to my nice family!

I return home to my beloved ones.

Oh, to my beloved ones!

Who are loving me

with all the warmth of their hearts.

Who are coming running

when I am opening the door.

To smile at me,

to embrace me,

to let me in

in their home and in their hearts, too.

Oh, and in their hearts, too!

Me – the stranger and scavenger of love

I am.

Who is passing by their windows at night

in a bus.

Dreaming about living their nice lives

in *The Prau*.

**a cynical cat collector at work at 4 a.m.
[Bonus]**

at night

sitting in the dark

pissing

listening to another pussy

in heat

out in the cold

crying

like a thrashed-trashed heart-broken
butchered juicy piece of junk cunt

we all want to be

victims

don't we my love

makes everything

easier

especially

pissing in the dark after the job

is finally

done

right

my little princess out in the cold

at night

doing your job

in

the dark

3rd Album

サクラ

SEA ME

The Ballad of Ōka the Sea Creature

When I was young

I was used to be a bird of prey.

Once

soaring high

I came crashing down with deadly speed

to kill, destroy, erase.

But just before finishing off my victim

once and for all

they got me

and I fell prey myself.

I hit the waves

and went immediately under

with my pilot.

The sea overwhelmed us,

claiming me and him.

He tried to fight the sea,

he tried to fight me,

he tried to save himself.

Weakened already

by a wound too many

he was losing the fight

by losing conciseness.

All seemed lost

until she came.

Staring first at me and then at him

full of curiosity

the sea creature made her decision

fast.

It was love at first sight.

She ripped off the canopy

and pulled him

out and off

she went with him.

Leaving me behind to sink

deeper

and deeper to meet

my fate.

I watched her

 taking him to the island nearby,

taking him to safety.

I was heartbroken.

But I was happy at the same time

for him

(and for her as well).

After dragging him on the shore

she slipped back into her element

to watch him from afar

with longing in her eyes.

All seemed well at last,

when suddenly another bird of prey

turned up and swooped down on him

with a vengeance.

She erupted in a scream

and rushed ashore to save him again,

but was merciless

cut down in a burst of bullets.

Sinking to the bottom of the sea

I watched them dying

crying my heart out.

Sitting there ever since

the sea became part of me

and I became part of the sea.

Dreaming about the time

when I was young

and became a bird of death.

Siren's Call Aftermath

Arriving at my destination at last

I am standing on the beach

Standing there

after losing everything

I am finally losing it

and call out in despair

Howling

before after until

I scream

And a head appears above the waves

bobbing up and down

staring at me with lovely eyes full of
sadness

Mirroring her sadness

I smile

knowing that in any sample of sadness

is a bit of madness

waiting to be set free

The endearing creature is riding the waves

and comes ashore

Reaching out

I am touching her lovely face

Tracing the outline of her destiny

I am outlining my own fate

Mirroring my madness

she smiles back

Slashing my wits in a twist of fate

I see the twist of fate

create a new one

And her lovely face turns to heaven

where I am drifting like a dead leaf

in an ocean of clouds

But graced by a school of cherry blossoms

I slash my wrists in another twist of fate

again

Landing hard after flying so high

I am stranded

again

in her embrace

Snuggled into her bosom

I am gazing at her

lovely features

Waiting expectantly

She just smiles

again

and drinks my lust

Dream Diver

Still dripping wet from a shallow dream

I jump right of its edge

into a deeper one.

Reaching out to the sun's lovely face

I catch a cherry blossom

dancing in the summer breeze.

Smiling

while turning into a siren

she sinks her fangs into my neck.

Feasting on me

she drags me deeper and

deeper into her embrace.

Stunned

I am stumbling deeper and

deeper.

Gliding

through her black abyss.

Gliding

into oblivion

where wrecked dreams come to crash.

Ground Zero

He knew

my look was a promise.

And so

his was a promise in return.

For sure.

My promise was

to show him the way to rainbow's end.

And so

his was to find me there.

So

off I went

and arrived

at rainbow's end at

a castle made of light and air.

Making it

a home for us

I started to wait

for him.

While the light

burning brighter by the second

was burning this very home

into shadows and dusk,

I did hold out

for him.

Withering away much too slowly

I wept

'til my tears turned ashen, too.

It was a test.

For sure.

But

who failed whom?

Who fooled whom?

Gone

I follow the trail of decaying

cherry blossoms to her place.

I don't know why.

Step by step

I follow the withering trail

she left behind for me.

But why?

With every step I take closer to her home

the landscape around me takes a step back.

No.

It dissolves right under my feet

and leaves nothing behind.

When I reach the threshold to her dream

I don't stop but keep walking.

Still not knowing what's going on

I am crossing over.

When I finally reach the shore of her
nightmares

I don't stop but walk right into the waves

that

aren't anymore.

Like her place,

her home,

her dream

aren't any longer.

Nothing but shadows

burnt into the ground

to behold.

But then I look up and around:

Wasn't there a noise?

A sound somewhere?

I listen carefully.

I listen hard.

But there is nothing.

Nothing

but the fading echo of a memory of

a siren's call.

In Memoriam

Remember (the time)

when we were flying so high

we were falling instead of rising?

Remember (the time)

when our lover's embrace

made us strangers?

Remember (the time)

when a sea of cherry blossoms

became a desert of death?

Remember (the time)

when HAPPINESS was spelled

SUFFERING?

(Those were the times, right?)

You do remember (them),

don't you?

Sleeping

in your Paulownia casket.

Crying out.

Screaming.

Dying

over and over

again

in your sleepless dreams.

Dismembered

I wake up

surrounded by trees.

They remind me of home:

How beautiful were the cherry trees

in our garden

back then.

How lovely where the cherry blossoms

when spring came around.

How lovely they are

now!

But then

an old man comes around.

Looking at me full of sorrow and sadness

he says: "Take a closer look, child!

Those ain't no cherry trees.

No, they ain't."

I do and wake

up

in

a casket garden.

She Was [Bonus]

at the museum

when the lights are on

looking at a certain painting on the wall

all

I see

is a shadow of a ghost

dead eyes

in a hollowed face

framed by an emptied smile

crowned by ashen hair

with a decomposing cherry blossom

tugged behind one ear

wings spread wide to strike

to prey

upon

me

a ghost of a shadow

is

all I see

glaring back at me in front of the mirror

when the lights are off

at home

Credits

Chrysalis & Orchid

Idea: on the 2nd of July 2013.

Written in Seoul: between the 2nd and 4th of July 2013.

Thanks: to the movies "Go" and "Virgin Snow"; to the bands Vidulgi OoyoO, SmackSoft, Romantiqua, Hellivision, Aurorasting, Baby Animals, Camel, Black Sabbath and Jethro Tull; to the Salon Badabie; to Dirk Schlottmann; to Brian K. Vaughan & Fiona Staples and to John Shirley.

The Prau

Idea: on the 19th of February 2017.

Written in Cheongju, Seoul and Kunsan: between the 19th and the 25th of February 2017.

Thanks: to Adnan Alam, Dr. Joachim Wittkowski, Prof. Dr. Heinz H. Menge, Werner Boschmann, Detlef Wagenschütz and Ilse Wagenschütz; to all the people working at A Twosome Place (Tiger Plaza, KU, Seoul), to all the people working at Deoksugung Shop & Cafe Doldamgil (Deoksugung, Seoul) and to all the people working at What The Book? (Itaewon, Seoul); to the movies "your name.", "Virgin Snow" and "Into The Night"; to the bands and musicians Jethro Tull, The Who, Deep Purple, Rory Gallagher, Kasabian, RADWIMPS, Justin Hurwitz and Leonard Cohen; to Krys Lee, Dan Wells, Ira B. Nadel, John B. Duncan, Nathan Edmondson & Phil Noto, Ingeborg Bachmann and Paul Celan and a special thanks to the condominium *The Prau* at the outskirts of Seoul.

サクラ

Idea: on the 15th of April 2017.

Written in Seoul and Suwon: between the 15th of April 2017 and the 5th of May 2017.

Thanks: to the exhibitions "Bring Them Home" (National Museum of Contemporary Korean History, Seoul) and "When Art Becomes Liberty: The Egyptian Surrealists (1938-1945)" (MMCA, Deoksugung, Seoul); to the airplane Yokosuka MXY-7; to the bands and musicians Dismember, Runemagick, And Then She Came, Royal Hunt, RADWIMPS, The Who, Leonard Cohen, Rainbow, Dio, Deep Purple und Jethro Tull; to the movies "your name.", "A Good Rain Knows", "Blue Submarine No. 6", "Oblivion", "Die kleine Meerjungfrau" (ČSSR 1976) and "Goya – oder der arge Weg der Erkenntnis"; to the comic series "Birds of Prey"; to Tsugumi Ohba & Takeshi Obata, Michael Buckley and Paul Celan; to Francisco de Goya; to Konrad Wolf; to all the places where this album was written – especially thanks to Coffee Boo in Suwon and in Seoul to Deoksugung Shop & Cafe Doldamgil and to A Twosome Place, Tiger Plaza, KU.

a tree at day

at night a dragon